The Ties We Weave

A Collection of Poems on Family, Friendship, and Self-Love

Sunitha Nair

BookLeaf Publishing

India | USA | UK

Made with ❤ on the BookLeaf Publishing Platform
www.bookleafpub.in
www.bookleafpub.com

Dedication

To those who stood by me through every high and low.
To my Dad, my constant source of inspiration.
To Amma and Kuttan, my heart's greatest comfort.
To Krish and Ishu, who support me in every journey I take.
To God, my guiding light.

Preface

This book is a reflection of my observations of the people around me and how they have influenced my life in different ways. Some poems explore self-doubt and self-love, capturing the complexities of being human. Others evoke various emotions, each shaped by the mood in which they were written. Many lines come to me spontaneously as I sit and ponder the intricacies of life. My writing is deeply influenced by the people, things, situations, and moods I encounter, shaping each piece with a unique perspective.

"Life is meant to be lived, not simply as it is."

Acknowledgements

Writing this book has been a journey of emotions, reflections, and deep gratitude. Each poem is a piece of my heart, shaped by the people and moments that have touched my life.

To my family, thank you for your unwavering love and support. Your presence has been my greatest comfort, and your encouragement has given me the strength to express my thoughts through words.

To my friends, you are the laughter in my happiest moments and the solace in my darkest days. Your kindness, honesty, and companionship have inspired many of these poems, and I am endlessly grateful for the memories we share.

To the self—the part of me that has doubted, healed, and learned to love again—this collection is a reminder that growth is a journey, and every emotion is worth embracing.

And finally, to every reader who picks up this book, thank you. May these words resonate with you, remind you of love in all its forms, and bring you comfort in moments of solitude.

1. Sense Of Achievement

For a girl child taking her first breath,
A life embraced, defying death.
A world that welcomes, yet resists,
Her very birth—an achievement exists.

For the poor, a simple delight,
Three meals a day, a dream in sight.
A luxury rare, yet deeply profound,
A victory won without a sound.

For the ambitious, chasing high,
A home, a car, a future to buy.
Success measured in what they own,
Yet built on dreams once unknown.

For a father, joy takes form,
In giving before the need is born.
A silent hero, strong and true,
His love reflected in all they do.

For a mother, torn yet whole,
A life of balance, a giving soul.
Supermom, super wife, she strives,
Juggling roles, yet love survives.

For the leader, words once sworn,
Turn to deeds—his promise borne.
Not for power, not for fame,
But for the trust upon his name.

And for me, the path unclear,
Achievement still feels nowhere near.
But is it measured in the grand and vast?
Or hidden in moments that simply passed?

So tell me now, if you may,
What is achievement, day by day?
Is it reaching heights unknown,
Or finding meaning in seeds we've sown?

2. Caged Strength

Her eyes sparkled, fierce and bright,
A fire within, a warrior's light.
She walked for miles, through dust and stone,
With steady steps, yet all alone.

She dared not stop, nor take a breath,
For fear they'd call her pause a death.
Weakness was not hers to claim,
So she kept walking, fueled by flame.

But as she turned to taste the sky,
Chains of love made her ask why.
Miles ahead, yet bound so tight,
Her own held her from taking flight.

3. Black Coffee

Black coffee in my hand, so warm, so deep,
A fragrance that lingers, a memory to keep.
Each sip takes me back to a time so sweet,
When the world slowed down, with hearts that would
meet.

The steam in the air, the quiet, the glow,
The moments we shared, just us, in the flow.
Your smile, your laughter, the calm in your eyes,
As we drank in the silence, beneath the sky.

The rich, bold flavor, so bitter, yet kind,
It brings me to you, every time I unwind.
Black coffee, a memory, forever to stay,
Of love, of us, in the sweetest of ways.

4. Where I Belong

I want to be lost in a place beyond sight,
Where silence embraces, and shadows feel light.

I want to be found where my soul once knew,
The peace of the past, where my spirit grew.

I want to be at peace where my mind runs free,
Where creativity flows like the endless sea.

I want to create where change takes flight,
Where dreams turn real, and dark turns bright.

And through it all, in every space,
I hope life meets me with gentle grace.

5. Those Days

Those days feel good when the sun shines bright,
And just as sweet when rain pours with might.

Those days are warm when I stay in bed,
And strong when I rise, with dreams widespread.

Those days are beautiful with loved ones near,
Yet just as peaceful when I'm my own seer.
I've lived through all, the highs and lows,
Yet a hollow space within me grows.

Perhaps, somewhere on paths unseen,
More of *those days* are yet to be seen.

6. Love Me Like This

Love me with all your heart,
Like the scent of old books, whispering stories untold,
Like the earth after rain, fresh and bold,
Like the steam of tea, warm and deep,
Like the sun that rises from a golden sleep.

Love me in a way untouched by time,
Like a feeling never traced, never defined.

7. Lost Melody

When was the last time I sang out loud?
When did my voice rise, clear and proud?
I asked myself, but all I found—
A silence where my song once drowned.

I searched my mind for notes once bright,
But all I heard was a hum in flight.
A borrowed tune, not truly mine,
A distant echo lost in time.

Have I forgotten how to sing?
Or did life quiet everything?

8. A Father's Love

In the quiet hours, he stands so tall,
With sacrifices unseen, he gives his all.
Through the struggles, through the years,
His love for us shines, wiping all fears.

A heart that gives without a sound,
In his embrace, strength is found.
He works, he gives, and asks for none,
All for the family, he's second to none.

His love is the anchor, the steady guide,
In every storm, he's by our side.
With every sacrifice, his heart does show,
A father's love, that continues to grow.

Through sleepless nights and weary days,
He lights our paths in countless ways.
A hero without a cape or crown,
His love for us never lets us down.

So here's to Dad, with love so true,
For all you've done, and all you do.

9. Embracing Me

In the quiet of my soul, I find my grace,
A gentle light, a peaceful space.
Through spirituality, I learn to see,
The love I seek begins with me.

I honor my heart, my mind, my soul,
In every thought, I make me whole.
With self-care as my guiding star,
I heal, I grow, and go so far.

No longer bound by fear or doubt,
I listen to my heart, let it shout.
For in this love, I see my worth,
A sacred journey, a new rebirth.

Through stillness and breath, I find my peace,
In each moment, my joys increase.
I nurture my spirit, tender and true,
And in that care, I am renewed.

In the mirror of my mind, I see,
The beauty that is meant to be.
With self-love, I gently repair,
And thrive in spirituality and self-care.

10. Wandering Souls

I travel to places unknown and wide,
Where cultures bloom, and hearts collide.
In every smile, a story unfolds,
A tapestry of life, rich and bold.

The sacred lands, where peace is found,
Whispering wisdom without a sound.
Awed by the people, their grace and light,
Their spirit guides me through the night.

New paths I tread, with open eyes,
Embracing the world, beneath the skies.
In every journey, I find my way,
A deeper connection, every day.

11. Miles-apart bonds

Across the miles, our hearts still stay,
Picking up where we left off, day by day.
The laughter echoes, the secrets we share,
In every memory, you're still right there.

We remember the moments, the joy and the tears,
The whispered stories, the silly fears.
In the quiet, we feel each other's grace,
A friendship that time cannot erase.

Though distance may part us, you're never far,
Your spirit with me, like a guiding star.
We respect each other, with love we grow,
For in each memory, our bond will glow.

12. A Mother's Journey

She wakes before the morning light,
Soft hands weaving day from night.
A gentle touch, a loving gaze,
Her life a song of endless days.

She feeds, she mends, she holds, she stays,
Her dreams set aside in quiet ways.
She carries burdens, hides her pain,
Yet never lets her love wane.

Through sleepless nights and weary sighs,
She builds a world with sacrifice.
Her hands may tremble, her steps may slow,
Yet in her heart, love still flows.

Then time, like wind, begins to shift,
Her nest now quiet, the air adrift.
She looks around, a world unknown,
No longer just a home she's sown.

For years she gave, now life returns,
A fire within her gently burns.
To walk new paths, to breathe, to see,
To claim the joy she once set free.

Her health, her dreams, her laughter bright,
Deserve the love she gave in light.
For a mother's life is more than giving—
It's knowing she, too, is worth living.

13. The Art of Watching

I sit in silence, eyes open wide,
A quiet observer, time on my side.
Faces pass like stories untold,
Expressions whisper, secrets unfold.

A furrowed brow, a fleeting sigh,
A restless foot, a distant eye.
Laughter ringing, sorrow concealed,
Emotions unspoken, yet all revealed.

The world moves fast, yet I stay still,
Drinking in life, bending at will.
The rustling leaves, the dancing breeze,
The silent hum of swaying trees.

A child's wonder, an elder's gaze,
A lover's longing, a dreamer's haze.
Every glance, a tale it weaves,
Written in the way one breathes.

To sit, to watch, to simply be,
To read the world as poetry.
Not lost in rush, nor trapped in time,
Just feeling life in its own rhyme.

14. Between the Pages

I lose myself in pages deep,
Where stories wake and secrets sleep.
A whispered tale, a world unseen,
A fleeting thought, a golden dream.

The rustling paper sings to me,
Of magic lands and endless seas.
Heroes rise and kingdoms fall,
I live a thousand lives in all.

By candle's glow or morning light,
Each word takes wings, takes fearless flight.
A pirate's quest, a poet's sigh,
A love that blooms, a last goodbye.

I dream in ink, I breathe in lines,
Each chapter's turn, a fate entwined.
No place too far, no time too late,
For books unlock the hands of fate.

And when the world feels cold and small,
I find my home inside them all.

15. My Angel, My Love

When darkness loomed and hope was gone,
You stepped in, like the break of dawn.
A gentle touch, a whispered cheer,
You wiped away each fallen tear.

I had surrendered, lost and cold,
But you breathed warmth into my soul.
With every word, with every glance,
You gave my weary heart a chance.

Through storms and trials, highs and lows,
Your love's the light that always glows.
With every step, you stand so near,
My guiding star, my love sincere.

Not just a man, but heaven-sent,
A gift of love, my heart's lament.
My angel here, my sweetest part,
You are the wings around my heart.

16. Whispers of the Mountains

I wander where the mountains rise,
Beneath the ever-changing skies.
Where dawn ignites the world in gold,
And silent peaks their secrets hold.

The morning air, so crisp, so free,
Whispers ancient songs to me.
With every path, with every climb,
I lose myself and step through time.

In temples old, in sacred light,
I find my soul, I feel so right.
The chants, the bells, the incense near,
Bring peace that drowns out doubt and fear.

Through winding roads, through distant lands,
I greet the world with open hands.
I meet its people, share their ways,
Their simple joys, their quiet days.

Each journey carves into my soul,
A story new, a heart made whole.
For as I roam, I come to see,
The world unfolds the best in me.

17. The Child I Was

I tried to fit, to laugh, to blend,
To be the one they called a friend.
But every joke, each word they said,
Lived like echoes in my head.

Was I too loud, or much too shy?
Would they notice if I tried?
A step too close, a step too far,
In their world, I was a scar.

At home, I fought with words of fire,
My heart a storm, my thoughts a wire.
Why don't they see? Why can't they hear?
The weight I carried, the silent fear.

Each rule, each "no," each slammed-shut door,
Made me want to scream some more.
A tangled web of right and wrong,
A child lost, yet craving strong.

And yet, in time, I came to see,
The war was not the world—it was in me.
The fears, the fights, the restless tide,
Were echoes of a heart untried.

Now looking back, I understand,
The child I was still holds my hand.
Not lost, not weak, not wrong, not small—
Just learning how to stand at all.

18. Threads Across the Miles

Scattered far, yet hearts still near,
We meet in calls, in laughs sincere.
Between the work, the daily race,
We find our time, we hold our space.

No longer kids, yet still the same,
Old nicknames spark, we play the game.
Stories shared of life's new bends,
Of jobs, of love, of far-off ends.

In cafes bright or midnight chats,
We bridge the gaps with words and laughs.
Miles may stretch, but bonds don't break,
For real friends time can never take.

19. A Daughter's Worry

Their voices now are soft and slow,
Their steps not steady as they go.
The hands that once held mine so tight,
Now tremble softly in the night.

Miles away, yet close in thought,
Their every need, my heart has caught.
Are they eating? Are they well?
Do they hide the aches they never tell?

The house is quiet, the rooms feel cold,
Once filled with love, now growing old.
The laughter fades, the days grow long,
Yet they still smile, they still stay strong.

How do I care? How do I stay?
When life has pulled me far away?
A call, a visit, love so true,
Yet never feels like quite enough to do.

I pray they know, I hope they see,
That every breath, they live in me.
And though apart, my heart won't roam,
For they will always be my home.

20. New Roads, Same Heart

You pack your bags, a brand-new start,
But take a piece—my love, my heart.
A different place, a life unknown,
Yet still, you'll never be alone.

You'll learn to cook, you'll find your way,
Meet new faces, bright your days.
But will you miss our little space?
The laughter, love, our warm embrace?

I worry, love, but trust you too,
For every step, I walk with you.
No miles can shake what we have grown,
No place will ever be **not** home.

21. The Midway Mark

We stand between the then and now,
With lines of time upon our brow.
The dreams of youth, the weight of years,
A heart that's strong, yet full of fears.

We've built our lives, we've loved, we've lost,
We've learned what every choice has cost.
Careers, commitments, restless nights,
The silent battles, unseen fights.

Yet in this age, there's beauty too,
A wiser heart, a broader view.
The rush has slowed, yet joy runs deep,
In love we give, in bonds we keep.

The past may call, but we stand tall,
With space to grow, with room to fall.
The road ahead is still unknown,
But we are more than flesh and bone.

For every dream that still survives,
For love, for laughter, burning bright—
The best may yet be on its way,
The golden years, the softer light.